WRITING
WITHOUT
THE MUSE

WRITING

WITHOUT

THE MUSE

60 Beginning Exercises
for the Creative Writer

New and Revised Edition
by Beth Baruch Joselow

STORY LINE PRESS   1999

Published by Story Line Press, Three Oaks Farm, PO Box 1240, Ashland, OR 97520-0055

This publication was made possible thanks in part to the generous support of the Nicholas Roerich Museum, the Andrew W. Mellon Foundation, the National Endowment for the Arts, and our individual contributors.

Text design by Chiquita Babb
Cover design by Lysa McDowell
Cover painting by Marc Chagall, "Le Vent dans les Fleurs au Clair de Lune"
© 1999 Artists Rights Society (ARS), New York / ADAGP, Paris

Library of Congress Cataloging-in-Publication Data

Joselow, Beth.
    Writing without the muse : 60 beginning exercises for the creative writer / by Beth Baruch Joselow — New and rev. ed.
        p.   cm. — (Story Line Press writers' guide)

        ISBN 1-885266-73-1 (alk. paper)
        1. English language—Rhetoric—Problems, exercises, etc.
        2. Creative writing—Problems, Exercises, etc. I. Title.
        II. Series: Writers' guide.
        PE1413.J65   1999
        808'.042'076—dc21   98-54227
                                    CIP

CONTENTS

WRITING
WITHOUT
THE MUSE

INTRODUCTION

You want to write, but you don't know where to begin. You think it must be easy for some people to sit down at a desk and get going, but for you the blank page stays blank. Where do writers get their ideas? How do they know where they're going? You're not even sure where you *want* to go.

Sometimes the hardest part of writing is just getting started. I hope the ideas in this book will help get you on your way. The good news is, even if you don't know where you're going you can still end up someplace that's worth the trip. And you can have a good time getting there.

This book is a compilation of exercises I have used with writing classes over the past 15 years. This second edition incorporates ten new exercises: five poetry exercises especially for elementary school age children (but challenging at any age), and five which I recommend for those who want most to record, or make use of, their own memories.

Many of the exercises are meant to help beginning writers break out and examine the different elements of a piece of narrative writing, and to provide a means of practicing with one element at a time. Some exercises focus on dialogue, others on description, others on voice. Some are more general and are meant to stimulate ideas for characters and plot.

You do not have to work through these exercises in order. I'd suggest that you take a more personal tack and browse through them until you come across an idea you would like to try.

Some of these activities, such as journal writing, are things you may wish to incorporate into a daily or weekly routine of writing. Writing is like any other skill — the more you practice, the better you'll become, and the easier it will seem.

Do plan to write several times a week, to keep the engine well-oiled. If that seems intimidating, begin by strictly limiting your writing time. Stick to your rule — that you will write for 20 minutes three times a week. Several short sessions should be easy to accomplish in a week — easier, perhaps, than one long session of a couple of hours. You will find that regular, short writing sessions can be very productive, and less intimidating than long hours in front of a blank screen or page. When your ideas begin to take off, you will want to put more time into each session, but let that occur naturally. For right now, remember that if you come up with only one paragraph, or even one sentence or a single line of a poem, it will be more than you have been getting on paper previously. That's a start, and a start is all you need.

Some of the ideas in this book may be useful one time only to help you explore new territory. Others may be adopted as writing habits that you'll come to rely on for ready inspiration and fuel. In many cases, you may wish to try your own variations. These are only suggestions, culled from assignments my students have made good use of over the years and from experiments and exercises that have been helpful to me in my own writing. Like athletes, writers can always use a good warm-up.

And now for a few important truths:

1. There is *never* a time when you have nothing to say. You just need to find where it is. Carry a pocket notebook at all times. Get into the habit of noting things, seeing them with an eye for detail. Write down bits of overheard dialogue. Describe interesting looking people, places, things, tastes, sounds. This is not just practice, it is material you can store for dry spells. But even if you never make concrete use of your notes, you will be developing habits of observation that will serve your writing well.

2. You can make anything new. There is no such thing as a story that's been told too many times. Point of view makes the difference. You have a unique point of view and it will show up in your writing, especially as you develop the habit of writing regularly.

3. It's helpful to have a particular place in your home where you do your writing. Somehow this habit seems to stimulate regular writing by imprinting the message that when you are in this place it is time to write — that's the Pavlovian effect. Take advantage of it.

4. It doesn't matter whether you do your writing with a pencil and lined paper, or on a computer screen. Experiment with different tools for writing until you find the one that feels most comfortable to you. I used to think that I could not possibly write at a keyboard; now I find it difficult to return to longhand. Try any method that strikes you — there's no need to feel locked in.

5. It's easier to change a piece of writing than it is to change most works of art, so try anything you like, even if it seems silly at first. When you have enjoyed the process of writing, your audience is more likely to enjoy what you have written.

This book has been constructed as simply as possible, to encourage you to pick it up freely, as if it's light, not heavy.

Words are there to be played with. Writing is *creative* work. Play is an important part of creativity. It's a mistake to approach the task of writing even a serious piece without some playfulness. Wonderful things can happen when you take the risk of just fooling around.

So give it a try. Surprise yourself. There's something lurking there that makes you want to write. Why not find out what it is.

WORKING FROM MEMORY

Most of us are interested in our own histories, and the histories of our families. We all have stories we like to tell about the past, and some that we prefer to mull over privately.

Often, people ask me for advice about how to get started on autobiographical writing. Even those who are natural story tellers have a hard time figuring out where to begin. It should be apparent that I don't believe that you ever have to start at the beginning. Begin wherever it occurs to you to begin. Later, you can give a shape to what you have written – whether that will be a chronological shape is entirely up to you.

I recommend that somewhere along the way you find and read an essay by Patricia Hampl, "Memory and Imagination." It is widely anthologized and appears for certain in a textbook published by Houghton-Mifflin, *The Dolphin Reader*. Hampl makes an excellent case for filling in the blanks of memory with a bit of imagination. It is impossible for anyone to remember enough of the details of a past experience to really make that story live on the page. She understands that the writer's mandate is to create a narrative that gives the reader the ability to *feel* what she remembers feeling – to experience the past along with the writer. That can happen only when enough details and description are provided. So, if you don't remember what color your first grade teacher wore on the first day of school, perhaps you do remember that she seemed very warm and friendly and you liked her immediately. Maybe it wasn't a sunny yellow dress, but if you use that description, you may help the reader join you in your memories.

Following are some possible places for you to start to record the story of your life. Some of the exercises are more focussed versions of the exercises in the next section of this book. I hope they are helpful.

Exercise 1

PORTRAITS

I t may be easier to begin to write about your life by beginning with the people who play important roles for you. Parents are an obvious first choice, but, of course, you may have many others.

Create a portrait of a person who has been important to you. Ask yourself the following questions as you get started:

1. Write down the first five characteristics that come to mind when you think about this person.

2. Explain the prominence of each of these characteristics: why does it stand out?

3. How have you been influenced by this person?

4. What have you missed in this relationship – what would you like to make different in it?

5. Briefly outline a story about this person that seems to reveal his/her character at its:

best
worst
most surprising
most typical
(Choose one or more of the above)

This should get you off to a good start. From here, try to complete a first draft that gives a full picture of this individual. This is one exercise that will very much benefit from having a reader take a look at what you've written and offer comments for your next draft. Ask your reader to let you know what might be missing from the portrait, what needs more explanation.

Exercise 2

WHAT I LOVE

We do not often put into words exactly what we love about a favorite activity, or a favorite place. But such descriptions can be revealing and stimulating. Think about something (not a person) that means a great deal to you and with which you have long experience. Describe for an interested audience what it is that makes this activity or object or place so special.

Exercise 3

THEN AND NOW

It may be that one of the things that makes writing the stories of our lives difficult is that our views change as we move on down the road. The boy you admired so much in high school seems shallow and superficial when you encounter him at the reunion. The ethics class you were forced to attend turns out to be the one you remember most, and feel most influenced by in your life today. The dull, quiet uncle is revealed to have a brilliant grasp of philosophy. He becomes tremendously appealing when you decide to study philosophy yourself. You begin to take long walks together, talking and talking.

That uncle would be a good subject for an exercise on then and now. Think of a person or an experience that you have changed your mind about in time. Describe how you used to feel, and contrast that with how you feel now. Take it one step further: see what you have to say about why your feelings have changed. Who are you now that is different from who you were before?

Exercise 4

YOUR PLACE IN HISTORY

Yes, like all of us, you have a place in history. Each of us can recall, often with surprising detail, where we were, what we were doing when we first heard of some major moment (usually a crisis, alas) in history. It might be the Challenger space shuttle disaster, or the day Martin Luther King was shot, or the day Richard Nixon resigned. It could be the night we first watched a man walk on the moon.

In a sense, you have been an eyewitness to many significant events. I remember standing in the kitchen with my mother, still in my school clothes after dinner, a striped cotton dish towel in my hand. I stared down at my saddle shoes and white socks, listening intently while President Kennedy spoke on the radio of the Cuban missile crisis. My heart pounded. I thought we would soon be at war.

I was in the kitchen again, my own kitchen this time, when a friend knocked frantically at the back door to tell me that John Lennon had been shot. I suppose I could write a piece that took advantage of the odd juxtaposition of the most ordinary, least dramatic room in the house being the setting for several different announcements of startling news. If you feel that you have no dramatic events in your life, write yourself into some of the historical moments that have taken place in the last several years.

Where were you when...? Tell us. Give us the details.

Exercise 5

A BUNCH OF GOOD IDEAS

This is really a bonus exercise, full of good ideas, courtesy of my students at The Corcoran School of Art, who held a brainstorming session on ideas for autobiographical writing. Many of these could begin as journal entries that can be expanded.

1. Moving…again
2. Parenting my pet
3. A portrait of my community (or communities)
4. My thoughts about Death, God
5. What I want my life to add up to
6. Ethical dilemmas
7. Small towns
8. A person or place seen in three separate moments
9. A portrait of a person in terms of where they meant to go and where they actually went
10. Sayings—what do they mean? Which ones are important to me?
11. My encounters with celebrities
12. Fame
13. What is home?
14. What do we need to know about our families and why?

15. What I think about money
16. Who is the black sheep in your family and why
17. Do we outgrow our childhood labels?
18. The myths/stories about our births
19. My relationship to the telephone
20. Songs of my family (my childhood)
21. Secrets
22. Inside/Outside: similarities and differences in my inner and outer self
23. Violence in our culture
24. Describe a tradition and your relationship to it
25. Write a letter to a future you
26. Describe a day at work
27. When have I felt most alive?
28. What am I most afraid of?
29. Favorite gifts I have gotten
30. Thoughts about time

HOW TO

PLAY WITH

WORDS

The following exercises are meant to be enjoyed. Think of them as a box of chocolates. Look for one that you expect will be delicious and take a bite. There is no special order to them. Poke around. See what appeals. Have fun. Remember: the best writing comes from enjoying the process of writing. It may be a struggle to get yourself started, but once you have a word or two on the page, let the games begin.

Exercise 6

RETELLING A TALE

A good way to learn about how a story is structured is to get inside of a familiar story and make some changes. Think of the story of Goldilocks and the Three Bears. Who tells the story as you remember it? Most tales that have come down to us through the oral tradition of storytelling are remembered in the voice of an anonymous narrator. When you change the voice and point of view, you inevitably change the narrative effect as well.

Pick a character (or an element such as the cottage, the porridge, Goldi's hair) from the story and let that character or element tell the story in its own voice.

A wonderful example of how original a story can be written through this method is the children's book titled *The True Story of The 3 Little Pigs By A. Wolf* as told to Jon Scieszka and illustrated by Lane Smith.

Exercise 7

FREEWRITING

I cannot imagine getting into a writing mode without freewriting. The idea of freewriting is a common one in writing classes these days, and it has become common because it works so reliably and so well.

Freewriting, or "automatic writing," is accomplished by simply writing without direction or goals in mind. Sit down in a comfortable spot with a clean piece of paper and a pen. Now, put your pen to the paper and start writing as fast as you can, *without thinking*. Write whatever words are in your mind, without thinking about sentences, grammar, spelling or any other structures. Keep up your speed so that you don't get stuck thinking about what you are saying. You are trying to let your subconscious mind guide you on this one.

Some people may wish to set a timer before they begin freewriting. Start with a 10-minute minimum. You will be able to fill at least a page in that time, if not more, if you are writing as quickly as you ought to be.

My own preference is to fill a page or two (my handwriting is relatively compact so I fit quite a bit onto one lined page of a notebook), rather than to time myself by the clock. Either way, *don't stop* until the time or the paper runs out. *Don't reread in the middle.*

Most likely you won't get any complete ideas from freewriting when you first experiment with it. Use it anyway, to relax yourself as you open a writing session. I find that if I start out with freewriting, my thoughts flow more smoothly when I really start to write out my ideas; words come more easily. I have overcome some of the anxieties I may have about writing, and have quieted the noise of the day, entering that contemplative space I need to inhabit in order to write.

Freewriting is the calesthenics of writing. Try to do a little freewriting several times a week to get yourself in shape, and to keep in shape. Even if it feels strange or silly to you at first, stick with it for a few weeks and see if you can make it click for you. For most people, it is a valuable tool.

You may not want to reread any of your freewriting for a while. If you do, it may seem nonsensical to you. You may wonder what use it has. Or you may find that you have surprised yourself by writing a beautiful phrase, or raising a topic that interests you. You may get an idea from what you have written in freewriting that can then be turned into a story, a memoir, an essay or a poem.

Exercise 8

ROOM WITH A VIEW

Choose a spot with a view that you like. It does not have to be scenic: you might like the view from a certain table in a fast food place because it's a good vantage point for people watching. The place you choose may be quiet and bucolic, noisy and urban, indoors, outdoors, familiar, utterly new and unusual to you. Okay, once you've got your spot, sit there for fifteen minutes observing everything that you can take in. Use all five of your senses. How does the air there *feel*? What do you smell when you close your eyes? Or what do you imagine that you smell? Take notes as you make your observations. After you have spent a full fifteen minutes at your post, write a detailed sketch of the scene you have just taken in. You may want to do this right away, while your observations are freshly in mind. Or you may want to wait a day or two to let time do some sifting for you. Either way should give you something to work with.

Exercise 9

LEGITIMATE
EAVESDROPPING

Here's a legitimate excuse for eavesdropping. Plunk yourself down in a restaurant, on a bus, on a bench at a playground. Be sure to have your notebook with you because you are about to take notes on the conversations going on around you. Try to write down *exactly* what you hear. What you're looking for is real speech. Whether or not a story emerges from it is unimportant so far. If you have time, repeat your note-taking in different locales over a period of a few days. In five minutes you should be able to gather quite a bit of raw material. Sort through the conversations you have recorded. *Adding as little as possible to them*, create a poem or a narrative based on your notes. You may decide to combine things from different conversations, or to use one conversational fragment exactly as you heard it, letting it tell its own story. You are free to be as creative as you like with this, but *you may not change any of the words you heard spoken*, only the order of exchange, if necessary to your purpose.

Exercise 10

A PLACE ALTERED BY MOODS

$\mathbf{D}$escribe a place that you know well — a childhood bedroom, for example, or the kitchen you now use. Limit your description to about three paragraphs.

Now, describe the same place again, this time choosing a tone from the list below. Communicate this mood through your description. Repeat the exercise for as many qualities from the list as you like. (You may, if you wish, substitute a *person* you know well for a place you know well.)

Moods:

anger
love
boredom
anxiety
fear
impatience

shyness
condescension
nostalgia
happiness
desire
weariness
deceit
awe

Exercise 11

CHANGE VOICES

Write a descriptive piece, probably one or two pages long, describing your mother, or someone you know very, very well. In whatever fashion you wish, help us to really know what makes this person tick and what you think of her. Be specific. You should be writing from the view of someone *outside* this character; use the pronoun *she* or *he* in your description.

Next, write a second description of this person, this time in the person's own voice, using the pronoun *I*.

Exercise 12

OBSERVING A STRANGER

Take yourself to a busy public place — a park, a train station, a restaurant, a hospital lobby, a waiting room, the library — where you will inconspicuously observe the people around you and choose one person to focus on. Find someone who interests you and try to observe this person for at least twenty minutes. Then try to answer the following questions:

1. What is the person's physical appearance?
2. What is the person wearing?
3. What is this person's approximate age?
4. What do you think the person's occupation might be?
5. Where do you think this person might live? Why?
6. What kind of personality do you think this person might have (kind, sad, impatient, bossy, etc.)? What are the clues?
7. What other information can you come up with about this person?
   (Habits? married or single? children? friends? etc.)

You will need at least twenty minutes for thorough observation of a person. If your study is interrupted, you must choose a new person and begin again. You may follow your subject, as long as you remain inconspicuous. You may listen to any conversations the person may have, and may talk to your subject yourself, as long as you don't reveal your purpose.

Once you have answered the list of questons, write a character sketch or a brief biography of this person, including as much specific detail as possible. Later on, you may wish to attempt a story in which your newly created character figures prominently.

Exercise 13

A STORY YOU'VE TOLD A MILLION TIMES

R_emember that crazy time when....? You must have a stash of stories that you are tempted to tell at parties or when you are sitting around with friends. Chances are these stories have stuck with you because they are about something funny that happened, or something eerie, or something very moving, or something that remains hard to understand. Any of those qualities has to do with *tension*, and tension is the element that makes us want to read on, to find out what happens next.

Tell one of your tried and true stories. Write it for an anonymous reader. If you have trouble writing in your own voice, put the story in the mouth of one of the people in it. Let him or her tell the story. Does the story change when someone else tells it?

Exercise 14

STORIES FROM THE NEWSPAPER

Every day the newspaper is full of intriguing stories that are incomplete. What was that young girl doing out on the highway at 2:30 in the morning? Why did that team want to cross the Atlantic in a balloon? How could a long-term employee have embezzled so much money before being caught? What would it be like to live in a city that is regularly under siege?

Read the paper. Find a story that fascinates you — I mean really fascinates in a way that goes beyond mild interest. If it's an ongoing story, you may want to clip articles related to it over a period of time. If it involves a trial, you may want to go to the courthouse and sit in for a couple of hours. Observe the principal players. Now sit down and write about it. You should be able to enjoy answering all the questions that the newspaper stories leave unanswered. You will devise an interesting melange of truth and imagination.

Alternatively, take a headline only, and *without* reading the story, make up a story that fits the headline.

Exercise 15

GO OUTSIDE

Go outside. Find something unfamiliar — something growing in your garden, something living under a rock, something discarded in the alley. Bring it back to your desk. Observe it. Turn it around and look at it from all sides. Smell it. Listen to it. (You probably shouldn't taste it.) Touch it — what does it feel like? If it is not an animal, cut it open or tear it apart. What is revealed to you now? Write a 10-minute description of what you have found.

Now write it again, in a different voice — someone you know. A character from fiction. A celebrity. What would that person see that you don't? You may even elect to write in the voice of the object.

Exercise 16

ANSWERING A POEM

Leaf through a book of poems — an anthology, or a book by a poet you enjoy reading. Find a poem that appeals to you, one that uses fresh language, one that sounds musical when you read it aloud. Choose a poem that is at least 10 lines long.

Now you have some more choices:

A. Write an answer to the poem — a mirror-image poem, shaped as much like the one you have read as you can make it, made up of the thoughts you have in response to the original poem.

B. Cannibalize it. Pull out ten or 12 words or short phrases from the poem. Choose those that really appeal to you because they are unusual sounding, visually evocative, or strange. Work them into a poem of your own.

C. Take one line from the poem and use it as the first line for a poem of your own, one that need not resemble the original poem at all.

Exercise 17

LETTER FROM A PLACE YOU'VE NEVER BEEN

Imagine yourself on a journey to a place you have never visited before. It's striking! There are so many _____ . And the quality of the _____ is amazing! You've never seen anything that looked like the _____ . This is a place to write home about. Write a letter to someone you like, telling her all about your surroundings.

Exercise 18

ASSOCIATIONS

Think of the words "rainy day." Close your eyes and let yourself relax a bit, daydreaming with the phrase "rainy day" in mind. Now, quickly jot down ten associations you have with the words "rainy day." What does the phrase bring to mind? Memories? Feelings? Smells? Sounds? Write your list in note form, as quickly as you can.

Once it is complete, review your list and use one or more of the items on it as a jumping off point for a sketch or a story. One student of mine ended up writing a story in which a mud puddle figured prominently. See what your associations inspire.

You may also think of other potent phrases that evoke a lot of feelings and memories. Some examples of these might be *summer vacation, flying, family reunion, first day of school*. Think of some of your own and do an association list for them.

Exercise 19

INVENTIONS

The world is always in need of new inventions to make life easier, to solve economic, social or political problems, or simply to entertain us.

Dream up three inventions and write a brief description of each. They might be humorous, or they might be serious wishes for a product that solves a problem. They may be very realistic, or entirely fantastic. In mythology, for example, the cornucopia solves the problem of hunger and need. In real life, the aspirin has at least sometimes solved the problem of headaches!

Give each of your inventions a name. Then choose the one that interests you most and write an advertising brochure for it. What is going to sell this product? Convince me that I need it. Choose your words carefully. Advertising copy is terse, tightly written, and punchy, as whatever you write about your invention should be.

Exercise 20

MAKE IT NEW

Take an old, familiar story and think about how it might have developed differently. What if Cinderella never went to the ball?

What if Tom Sawyer lived in New York City? What if the South had won The Civil War? Write your version of what happens next.

Exercise 21

END IT FIRST

Sometimes it's hard to get started. Why do we think we must always begin at the beginning? Try writing an *ending* to a story. Don't worry yet about how things got to that point. Just think of an ending. For example:

After he repaired the broken wheel, Ted put it back on the bike and tightened it carefully. He picked up his backpack, hopped up on the worn seat and pedaled off. West this time.

— The End —

Write the story that got Ted onto that newly-fixed bike, heading West. Or think of an ending of your own, write it down, and then create a backward outline for the plot.

EXERCISE 22:
INTERNAL DIALOGUE

A good way to get to know a character is to get into a conversation with her.

Invent a character, or think of a character in a book you've read or a movie you've seen. You may also choose someone from history, or someone you actually know, or once knew. Begin by having the character make a provocative statement. For example:

AMELIA EARHART:

> *I'm so relieved that I've never been found. Life was much too public before I figured out a way to get lost.*

You can probably think of a few strong replies to such a statement. As they come to you, write your response:

ME:

> *Amelia, where have you been? We've been looking all over for you! Do you have any idea how many people have devoted themselves to trying to figure out what happened to you?*

And then:

AMELIA EARHART:

> *I was right here all the time! I went to work for Pan Am. Isn't that a hoot? I'll tell you how I did it....*

Go on from there. You can find out a lot about your character in even a brief exchange: What kind of vocabulary does she use? Does she have a sense of humor? Is she smart, wacky, happy, troubled, interested in other people? You may soon find, as I often do, that the character starts saying things before you know what they are going to be. After you've developed the dialogue for a while (two or three pages, perhaps), see if you have some ideas for settings and plots for this new person.

Exercise 23

A GRAB BAG OF OBJECTS

Gather an assortment of objects from around your house. Anything will do, although you may want to include some items that have some emotional resonance for you. Your selection might include a paperweight, a dustcloth, an ashtray, a shot glass, a crochet hook, a pocket knife — anything at all. When you have gathered a dozen or so things, put them into a bag. Then draw out four of them (or have someone else draw for you). No trades! What you draw is what you get. Now write a piece that incorporates these four objects as part of it. Some may have a prominent role; others may be background scenery only. The choice is yours.

Exercise 24

A GRAB BAG OF WORDS

J ust as you gathered a number of objects for a grab bag, you will this time gather *words*. Choose interesting words, and make sure you have a mixture of nouns and verbs. Examples of words that would do well on such a list include:

> Labrador retriever,
> garbage can,
> Rocky Mountains,
> soprano,
> subway, etc.

You may even want to throw in an adjective or an adverb if they are specific and descriptive enough (*sugary*, for example, or *furtively*). Write each word on a separate piece of paper and put them into a bag. Now draw out six words and, of course, write a piece that incorporates them.

Exercise 25

FAVORITE MEMORY

In addition to stories we tell often, we are all storehouses of significant memories that we have not tried, or not tried often, to voice. These may be fragments more than stories — the way you felt climbing the steep back stairs at your grandparents' house when you were small, the roommate you had for only three days in your first year at college. Leaf through your memories. Find one that is attractive to you, for reasons you do not need to understand. Write it out as precisely as you can. Give it an ending if it lacks one, or explore your feelings about what it means to you. Ask yourself why it would be interesting to someone else, and make it mean something to your reader.

Exercise 26

WRITING FROM PHOTO-GRAPHS AND PICTURES

P art of writing is trying to describe the pictures we see in our minds, so it is logical to practice that skill by looking at real photographs and artists' renderings. Choose a photograph from your family album or from a magazine. Or choose a painting or drawing that interests you, that has an element of mystery or tension, or a strong emotional atmosphere. Put yourself into the picture you have chosen and observe what goes on there. Make the people in the picture come to life. You may want to have one of them serve as the narrator as you tell their story — how they got there, or where they are going. When Stephen Sondheim tried this with a painting by Georges Seurat, the result was his award-winning musical, "Sunday in the Park With George."

Exercise 27
———

THE AIRPLANE

You are on an airplane. Your seatmate knows nothing about you when you strike up an ordinary conversation with each other. As he asks a few polite questions about the reason for your trip, where you're from, what you do, you have the opportunity to be anyone you like. You want to be:

> intriguing
> unprecedentedly boring
> unique
> an average Joe
> an adventurer
> a criminal
> a liar
> a social conscience
> a professional entertainer

You can be any of those things, or anything else you dream up. You have twenty minutes to tell your seatmate the story of your life.

Exercise 28

WRITING TO MUSIC

Explore the synergy between art forms by listening to music as you write — not keeping it on for background noise, but really listening to it. Begin with some soft music that you like, perhaps a piece that you've found to be soothing or relaxing in the past. See what happens when you write while listening, letting the music carry your thoughts with it, as a kind of freewriting. Experiment with different kinds of music. Do you think different thoughts when you play rock music, or patriotic music? What happens when you listen to songs sung in a language other than English? Try not to write about the music itself but to let your mood and your ideas be affected by it.

Exercise 29

CURRENT EVENTS

What's the world without a crisis? Think of a few world or national problems that are in the news right now. Pick an issue that really interests you — the disappearance of the ozone layer, the fight to control the spread of disease, the struggle of an emerging nation. What kind of character might be somehow affected by the issue you choose? His or her involvement may be deep, or very superficial, serious or humorous. The Cold War, for example, was the background for any number of humorous movies about some regular American family being stymied by unanticipated contact with a Russian they ended up liking. Can you use an issue in current news events as a jumping off point for a story?

Exercise 30

LOST THINGS

Make a list (I hope it's short) of things you have lost that were important to you. You may interpret the word "lost" as freely as you like. Choose one of the items on your list and write a piece explaining its importance to you, how it was lost, how your life was changed by its loss, or what you learned from losing it. If you wish, the lost item might become the centerpiecce in a story you attempt next. Thus, a symbol is born!

Exercise 31

THINK SMALL

Watching trapeze artists, I am always fascinated by the complexity of what they do. Every move they make is crucial, elegant, seemingly prolonged, although it may take only a second for a man to fly through the air to the strong, sure grasp of the partner who has swung out to meet him. Think of a small yet very full moment that you'd like to describe. Challenge yourself — don't make it too easy. You might think of baiting a fishhook, executing a dive, opening a bottle of champagne, pulling out of a parking space. Stick to something that takes about a minute. Then write a detailed, moment-to-moment description of that action. Let the reader see every bit of it.

Exercise 32

A SENTENCE FROM A BOOK

Close your eyes and open a novel or a book of short stories. Put your first finger on the page. Now open your eyes and record the sentence your finger has pointed out for you. That is your first sentence. Start writing. You are allowed three tries if the first sentence fate hands you is truly appalling. You may write either a poem or a story, whichever you feel most inspired to do.

Exercise 33

A LIST OF TITLES

This one is kind of like storing nuts for the winter. Set your thoughts on titles: titles for poems, titles for stories, titles for essays. Don't worry about developing the idea suggested by the title right now. Just think of interesting titles. "My Summer Vacation" is not an interesting title. "Going to Graceland" might be more interesting, for example, because it is more specific, and the words have an interesting *sound* in themselves due to their rhythm and the use of alliteration. But I'm sure you can do better than that one too. So make your titles intriguing. Think of ten or twelve. Now, keep that list in your writing notebook for use when you can't think of anything to write.

Exercise 34

COOKING WITH THE DICTIONARY

Writing is a lot like cooking. In the kitchen, a good cook can take a lot of familiar ingredients and put them together in new ways to invent a delicious new dish. Sometimes it's fun to just grab what's in the refrigerator and see what you can create. You can do that with writing too. The ingredients are words, of course. Set up a challenge for yourself by opening the dictionary at random and picking a word. Repeat that action until you have a list of a dozen words. Now — make a new dish, using all of the words on your list.

This exercise is a lot like doing a dot-to-dot picture. You are creating a kind of randomly composed map that will lead you to draw a complete picture. It could be interesting to use a specialized dictionary — a legal dictionary, or a dictionary of American slang terms. (One of my favorite dictionaries is *The Underworld Speaks*, a dictionary of criminal slang from 1935.)

Exercise 35

DREAM NOTEBOOK

Your creativity is at work every night, but most of us don't remember very much of what we dream. You can train yourself to remember more of your dreams very simply, by keeping a pen and paper right next to the bed and writing notes about your dreams the moment you wake up. As you begin to wake up, lie still, keeping your eyes closed. Pull your dream into your consciousness. Try writing without putting the lights on, with your eyes closed. Write just enough so that you will be able to jog your memory of the dream when you are more awake and can look at your notes. The point is to try to bring the dream into your consciousness as fully as you can before it completely flies away. If you do this regularly, you will find that you begin to remember more of your dreams and that you remember them more easily. Then you can make use of them, for settings, plots, emotional backgrounds, characters that spark stories and poems.

It is not important that you be absolutely accurate in writing down your dreams. If your imagination begins to go to work for you, don't worry about censoring it. Make use of it!

THE WRITER'S NOTEBOOK

I f you have not been keeping a notebook or a journal, it's time for you to get started with one. Find a notebook that is a convenient size for you to carry with you as often as possible. Choose a format that will make it easy for you to take notes, whether it's a small, spiral-bound notepad or a folded sheaf of papers that you put into a ring-binder or file folder at the end of each day. Carry a pen with you at all times, too.

Now, when you are hit with an idea for something you would like to think about, research, or write about, write it down in your notebook immediately. Use your notebook as well for writing down an interesting bit of dialogue you overhear, a musical line for a poem that pops into your head, or for doo-dling a description when you are waiting for a train, waiting for an appointment, or when you're stuck in traffic. People doodle pictures all the time — try doodling in words. Use your notebook to "talk" to yourself about ideas you are thinking of developing. Thinking changes when we write things down. Ideas develop in ways that don't occur when we keep our ideas silently to ourselves. These notes will remain your private notes, but by opening a kind of dialogue with the pages of your note-book, you will expand your thinking ability and be more pro-ductive. You will also be making a habit of writing, and that helps keep the writing engine oiled. Try to develop at least one idea from your notebook each week.

Exercise 37

THE FIVE SENSES

Get yourself a piece of fruit. If you like, you may go to the store and buy a fruit that you have never eaten before — how about a kiwi? A pomegranate? A mango? Now you are about to undertake a five-part experiment in writing.

1. *Look at* the fruit. Describe in as much detail as you can what you see. Think about its size, shape, color, texture, placement in its setting.

2. *Smell* the fruit and describe in detail what you smell.

3. *Touch and listen to* the piece of fruit. What does it feel like in your hands, against your fingertips? What do you hear when you rub its skin or shake it?

4. Finally, cut open the fruit and describe what it looks like inside. Now *taste* it, and describe in as much detail as you can what it tastes like.

Use all of these notes to write a finished, complete description of the fruit you select.

Exercise 38

TWO OBJECTS

This exercise will help you sharpen skills in making observations and comparisons. Make a study of two similar, yet not identical, objects. Some pairs that might work well for this purpose are:

a dog	a plush toy dog
a lemon	a plastic lemon
a watch	a clock
a rose	a tulip

Think of others that have similarities — and differences. Write down separate lists of similarities and differences. Now describe each of the objects as fully as possible by comparing it to the other in paragraph form. You may wish to add your emotional reaction to each of the objects as a final comparison.

Exercise 39

THE DINNER PARTY

Meals are occasions of ritual and psychological revelation — even meals taken alone. Think of some memorable occasions at the table. Thanksgiving is an obvious choice for a ritualized meal. You might think of other, similar occasions — birthday or anniversary celebrations, ethnic holidays. Or is there an ordinary meal, a breakfast or a dinner that you remember because something unusual happened that day? Think of one such occasion. Write about it, including descriptions of who was there, what was said, what the room looked like, how the table was set, what the weather outside was like, what you ate, what was *not* said. Be as inclusive as you can be. See if you can get the meal to tell a story.

Exercise 40

WRITING PARTNERS

Every writer should have a writing partner, or a writer's group. It is always helpful to have someone read what you've written and give you a reaction to it. The best way to share thoughts on material that is bound to be sensitive and personal, even if fictional, is to tell each other what you think works *best* in what is written. Then, you can offer a few comments or questions about things that are not working so well in the piece, or that the reader finds puzzling. A good critic doesn't so much poke holes in a piece as much as she finds its strengths and points them out to the writer, so that the writer may build upon them, rather than be discouraged. When I have been shown what is good about a piece, I am generally better prepared to accept suggestions about things that ought to be changed.

You and your partner or group should set up a regular time for meeting, so that you create a deadline for completing work. One group that I was in met every three weeks for about three hours. There were five of us in the group, so there was time to give everyone a fair amount of attention without any of us getting too tired out. We decided early on that no one was to bring anything too long. Longer pieces were to be distributed in advance of our meeting, so that the time together could be used for commentary rather than lengthy reading. We began our comments with praise, pointing out what worked well in what we had read. After everyone had said a few good words, we moved on to the questions we had about what did not seem to work so well in the piece. I got a lot of helpful advice this way. I also liked the fact that the members of my group were working on different kinds of things. It was interesting to have a novelist's perspective on a short story or a play, or to have a poet take a hard look at the novelist's sentences. We soon knew a lot about each other's strengths and weaknesses, as critics as well as writers, and were able to weigh the comments we received accordingly.

Knowing that you will be meeting once every third week, for example, will help you work to get things completed to show to your fellow writers. Each person should be given time to read work for the group and to hear comments about his work, so the group should remain relatively small if each person is to get a fair share of alert attention. And positively stated advice should be the golden rule.

It's possible to have a writing partner through the mail, and sometimes it is easier to give and receive criticism in writing rather than face-to-face. But at least for the early days of your writing career, I think it is much preferable to have a partner or a group that you meet with in person.

If you have not worked with your writing partner before, begin by interviewing each other in order to write a brief biographical sketch of one another. If you are part of a writer's group, all of the members of the group may do this exercise. Ask your partner interesting questions. If you already know a lot about her, you will be able to ask even more interesting questions, based on knowledge you already have. You are free to write your sketch of your partner in any tone or style you wish to adopt. But pointed satire is probably ill-advised!

Exercise 41

COLLABORATIONS

Collaborations are fun to do and can re-energize you just when you need a shot of originality.

With your writing partner, or another writer, set out some ground rules for a piece you will write together. Let's say that you will write responsive paragraphs. You begin by writing the first paragraph and passing it to your partner. Your partner writes a second paragraph and passes the two-paragraph piece back to you. You respond with a third paragraph, and so on. You may wish to decide at the outset how long the piece will be, or you may want to see where it takes you. This is an exercise that can be completed in one sitting, or that you can extend for weeks or months at a time. It's a perfect exercise for a pair of writers who are both on the computer Internet. There's a strong tradition of collaborative writing in theatre and film, and even in fiction and poetry writing. You may find that two heads are not only better than one, they may equal three!

Exercise 42

ACROSTICS

This simple idea should demonstrate to you how form helps free the writer — that it really doesn't restrict us. Sometimes just pinning yourself down to a strict method for composition helps sort out the scramble of ideas that result in your being stuck with no ideas that work for you.

Write someone's name or a word that may serve as your theme vertically down the side of a page. Write one line for each letter. See how closely you can relate the lines to each other, for example:

> Love in her eyes, she was
> Always there for Timmy,
> She was the most faithful friend,
> Smart, loyal, beautiful.
> I always wondered if I'd
> Ever have a dog like Lassie.

That's a pretty awful poem, but you get the idea. Now write a better one. Then think of other set-ups that will give you a grid to work on in composing a poem. Start every line with "I remember," or the letter M. Restrict yourself to 14 lines of 10 syllables each. Then you'll have written a kind of sonnet. Incidentally, you might want to look for a book of poetic forms and experiment with various forms, particularly the exotic ones that help emphasize the way in which writing can seem much like a game.

Exercise 43

THE DOOR IN THE WALL

Look at the wall next to where you are sitting. Now close your eyes and take several slow, deep breaths. Now imagine a door opening in that wall. What does the door look like? Is it big enough for an adult to walk through it, or only mouse-size? Is it decorated in any way? Old fashioned? Futuristic? Get a good handle on that door because you are about to open it and walk through it. Open the door, walk through it. Take your time. Write about everything you see there.

Exercise 44

EVERY DAY FOR A WEEK

Choose an experience that you have every day — eating breakfast, reading the newspaper, riding the subway, for example. Describe that same experience every day for a week or longer until you have a minimum of seven descriptions of the same activity. What is the difference in the descriptions? Have your descriptive techniques changed in that time? Have you begun to notice anything in the activity that you have not noticed before? Have you started to do things differently because you have become self-conscious about describing them? Are you more or less engaged with the activity you have described? This exercise should help you go deeper, to get at levels of experience that may have been unavailable to you because of the way we take the everyday for granted. If the exercise does not have that effect for you, you may wish to give it another try with a different activity.

Exercise 45

DICTATION

Speaking, as we will soon demonstrate, is not like writing. If you feel daunted by the blank page or the blank screen when you sit down to write, try talking to yourself. Tell your story into a tape recorder. Then transcribe it. You will be surprised how little talk it takes to fill a page — it's possible for 15 minutes of tape to fill ten pages or more — so keep your story short at first. Transcribe your story word for word — don't edit as you go. After you have the whole story on paper, rewrite it for sense and sentence structure. Feel free to add any embellishments you like.

Because writing is *not* transcribed speech, most writers cannot rely on tape recorders as a basic tool. But it is worth trying this exercise now and then, especially when you feel stuck or intimidated by a writing task.

Exercise 46

A MODERN MYTH

People of all cultures have created myths to explain the phenomena of their worlds. In our time, we rely on science to explain the mysterious and the profound for us. But what if we did away with the idea of science, or converted its mystique to real magic in our minds? How might we explain such things as monsoons or earthquakes then? The airplane? The television? The microwave? Write a contemporary myth to explain one such "magical" phenomenon from the world we inhabit.

Exercise 47

LETTERS THAT WILL NEVER BE SENT

Too often when it's time for me to write something I find myself procrastinating by writing a letter instead. "It's writing, isn't it?" I tell myself.

Yes, it is. But if we're going to stick to the task of doing "creative" writing, inventive writing, the letter has to be a creative endeavor. So, begin by choosing someone you would not ordinarily write to. Do you have something to say to an author of a book that has meant a lot to you? The director of a favorite film? A relative or a friend with whom you left certain important things unsaid? A former teacher? A colleague? A secret role model?

How are you going to persuade the imagined recipient to read your letter — all the way through? Be convincing. Adopt an attractive tone. Speak from your heart. (For an example of this exercise at its extreme see Stefan Zweig's novella, *Letter from an Unknown Woman*.)

Exercise 48

TWENTY QUESTIONS

It's time to start thinking about some of the questions that pop into your mind from time to time: Where did my ancestors live before they ended up in Hungary? Did Uncle Charles ever have an urgent dream in his life, or did he always feel content to manage a grocery store? What would it feel like to walk on the moon if you didn't need a space suit? What do ants think about? What would I be like if I'd become a film star?

In no time at all you should have a list of 20 or more such questions. Now pick one to answer — fully, of course, with lots of colorful detail. On another day you can answer another. Keep your list growing in your notebook.

Exercise 49

MIX AND MATCH

Drawing on people you know, people you don't "know" but observe often in your daily life, or familiar character types, make a list of five or more people and their usual surroundings. For example:

Precinct patrolman	his police car
Uncle Fritz	his tomato patch
Mr. Spock	the Starship Enterprise
Mrs. Adams	teller's booth at the bank
Lois Lane	newsroom at the Daily Planet

Now cut apart the elements of your list, separating the people from their surroundings. Make a pile of people and a pile of surroundings. Mix each pile up. Now, without looking, choose a person and a setting. Write about that person in his or her new setting. You may, if you wish, combine several people and settings in a series of related scenes.

Exercise 50

MAPS

Try mapping out a story, using either a real map or a map you make up. Circle five destinations on the real map, or draw a map that includes at least five destinations that you make up. It might look like this:

Gas station
Chicago, IL

Aunt Lula's back porch,
Harrisburg, PA

Amusement park
Orlando, Florida

Seminole Village
Miami, FL

Fishing boat
Gulfport, Mississippi

Draw lines between the destinations on your map. Now write your way from one to the other until you reach your final destination. Who is on this trip? Do they know why? See if you can let your characters reveal themselves to you as they travel.

Exercise 51

YOU ARE INVISIBLE

Okay, you're invisible. Where would you go? What would you be able to see that you can't see when you yourself are seen? Play out such a scene for yourself and thoroughly describe it in writing.

Exercise 52

CUT OUT EDITING

Take a piece that you have already written, preferably one that you are not quite satisfied with. Use a print-out, not a computer screen for this exercise. Put your pens and pencils away, too, and get out a pair of scissors. What can you do without in this story, memory, essay or fragment? Cut out all the words, phrases and sentences that now seem unnecessary to you. You are not allowed to add anything to the piece, you may only cut things out of it. What happens to the piece when you edit it by subtraction only?

Exercise 53

METAPHORICAL
THINKING

Sometimes the imagination needs a jump start to kick it over into the creative thinking side. Try making a list of metaphors and similes to propel your mind into the right channel for creative writing. You might begin by thinking of ten things that interest you and listing them down the left hand side of a page:

> Baseball
> Venus
> A waterfall
> Vampires
> Skiing
> A convertible
> South Africa
> The blues
> America
> Chocolate mousse

Begin a sentence with each of the items on your list followed by "is like..." Complete each sentence as imaginatively as you can. Next try substituting a descriptive word or phrase for the words on your list, or for words on a second list that you devise. For example:

snow = a cotton candy landscape

cactus garden = a yard full of prickly old men

Cousin Phil = the sad clown of the family

From your list, choose a sentence that you are very pleased with. Now develop that thought further for the length of a paragraph.

Is your thinking ready to follow another track now? Practicing an exercise like this one should make it easier for you to hop the fence between everyday and more creative thinking.

Exercise 54

IN THE MOMENT

Check out your five senses and write down your answers to the following questions *right now*:

What do I hear?
What do I smell?
What do I taste, or remember tasting right now?
What are the sensations on my skin?
What do I see?

What does all of this make me remember? think about? wish for?

Now write two pages (at least) based on being in the moment you are in *right now*.

Exercise 55

THE REPORTER

You have a lot of stories in your life that you can draw from when you are looking for writing ideas. So do your friends and relatives, and it is perfectly legitimate for you to use their stories as well.

Who do you know who is an interesting storyteller? Has someone close to you had an adventure you have enjoyed hearing about? A comic escapade? A sea change? Make a date to interview that person and to get the full story down in notes and/or on tape. Now write that story, with any embellishments you care to add.

(You can do this one again and again. Many writers have harvested stories from their families and towns: William Faulkner, Carson McCullers, Sherwood Anderson, Beth Henley are just a few famous examples.)

FIVE

EXERCISES

FOR CHILDREN

Children are natural poets. For the past several years, I have been poet-in-residence at Westbrook Elementary School in Montgomery County, Maryland. I've worked with some wonderful young writers there, in grades 1-5. With their help, I have experimented with using poetry to stimulate excitement about the writing process, and to provide a format for working on vocabulary, organization of ideas and editing skills.

Poetry does not have to be kept entirely separated from prose. It does not have to be scary, as it too often is for anybody who is more than 12 years old. I've also found that, despite the enormous popularity of talented humorous poets such as Jack Prelutsky and Shel Silverstein, children like all kinds of poems, not only the funny ones. What's more, they are eager to tackle poems that are not easy to understand at first glance. I've brought some rather adult poems, dense with wordplay and metaphor, to 10-year-olds who saw things in them that I had not yet discovered myself.

I love bringing poetry into the elementary school class-room. By making poems a normal part of the practice of writing, teachers can not only give their students a rewarding life-long interest, but they can take advantage of the form to work on all of the skills necessary for writing with grace and clarity.

I learned a great deal about how to structure poetry lessons for children from Kenneth Koch, whose outstanding books on teaching poetry to children are on my "must" list for teachers. *Rose, Where Did You Get That Red?* and *Wishes, Lies, and Dreams* are both in paperback and easy to find. The illustrated anthology of poems for young people, *Talking to the Sun*, edited by Koch and Kate Farrell is also a splendid source of poems that children respond to with enthusiasm.

Following are a few of the exercises that the Westbrook students have liked most over the years. Try them. You may like them!

Exercise 56

POEMS THAT ARE FUN TO SPEAK ALOUD

Each time I visit a classroom, I bring the students a poem or two to read and discuss. For this exercise for fourth or fifth grade students, we begin with a poem by the British poet, Gerard Manley Hopkins (1844-1889). After I read it aloud for the class, I sometimes ask everyone to read it aloud once more with me.

PIED BEAUTY

Glory be to God for dappled things —
    For skies of couple-colour as a brinded cow;
        For rose-moles all in stipple upon trout that swim;
Fresh-firecoal chestnut-falls; finches' wings;
    Landscape plotted and pieced — fold, fallow, and plough;
        and all trades, their gear and tackle and trim.
All things counter, original, spare, strange;
    Whatever is fickle, freckled (who knows how?)
        With swift, slow; sweet, sour; adazzle, dim;
He fathers-forth whose beauty is past change:
                Praise Him.

There is so much to discuss in this poem that we never get through all of it in just one session. The children often find it hard at first to understand the subject of the poem, so we begin by talking about the words themselves and the sounds that we find appealing. I ask students to choose a line or phrase that they especially like and to read it aloud. We talk about how our mouths feel when we say a line such as "Landscape plotted and pieced — fold, fallow, and plough." Then we might go on to talk about words we don't understand, with volunteers looking them up in the dictionary and reporting back to the class. We look for rhymes within lines as well as at the end of lines, and we point out alliterative phrases. By then we usually have come to some agreement about the meaning of this poem-hymn, and we are ready to write one of our own. I ask the students to aim for a rich vocabulary in their own hymns to nature, one that emphasizes the musical sounds of words. In the example below, a fourth grade student who is bi-lingual wrote his poem in Spanish and in English.

El RIO GRANDE

El mar es bello,
Y tambien la luna;
Me calma la tranquilidad
Del "Rio Grande;"
La noche es negra,
pero aqui hay una luz,
aqui, contigo, en la noche;
Todo esta bien,
con nostros aqui,
tu y yo, somos amigos.

THE RIO GRANDE

The sea is gorgeous
And so is the moon;

The tranquility of the "Rio Grande"
calms me;
the night is black,
but here is a light,
here, with you, in the night;
Everything's well,
with us here together,
you and I are friends

— *Julian Kurz*

Exercise 57

SOME VEGETABLE POEMS

I am grateful to Kenneth Koch for suggesting in one of his own books that an exercise could be built around the following poem.

from SOMEONE PUTS A PINEAPPLE TOGETHER

1. The hut stands by itself beneath the palms.
2. Out of their bottle the green geneii come.
3. A vine has climbed the other side of the wall.

4. The sea is spouting upward out of rocks.
5. The symbol of feasts and of oblivion…
6. White sky, pink sun, trees on a distant peak.

7. These lozenges are nailed up lattices.
8. The owl sits humped. It has a hundred eyes.
9. The coconut and cockerel in one.

10. This is how yesterday's volcano looks.
11. There is an island Palahude by name—
12. An uncivil shape like a gigantic haw.

— *Wallace Stevens*

There is a lot to talk about in this wonderful list of metaphors. I always bring a pineapple to the class and stand it prominently at the front of the room for the students to see. We go over each line of the poem, looking for what Stevens describes. I've yet to encounter a class that failed to take delight in seeing the pineapple as a rude noise, like "a gigantic haw," or one that couldn't see the green geneii freeing themselves from their bottle.

Once we have deciphered the poem to our satisfaction, and discussed the advantages of making metaphors while we are at it, I give each group of three or four students a fruit or vegetable of their own to examine and write about. At the supermarket, I will have looked for vegetables that the students are less familiar with, that are colorful and have interesting textures. Some of my favorites are eggplants, ginger root, bunches of beets, cauliflower, and acorn squash. Here are some of the poems we have grown from those beginnings.

LET'S IMAGINE...

(eggplant)

1. A green star shining in the sky
2. A green boat riding a violet wave
3. A purple bridge over troubled waters

4. Garbage spilling out of a bag
5. A cannon across enemy lines
6. A baby wrapped in a black blanket

7. A green hole in endless space
8. An aired football
9. A man in critical condition

10, As hollow as a dead man's skull
11. A black telephone
12. Thigh-master 9,000,000,000

— *Alex Tcherkassky*

GINGER ROOT

1. The hand of the old body
2. The cave turns off into many different passages
3. The old branch is finally dead
4. Maybe it's an old fossil
5. The one-eared one-horned man
6. Ten circles glued together
7. There seems to be a thumb on the top of this creature
8. Ants can enter in many ways
9. A water gun with many holes for water to shoot out
10. An old rotten potato

— *Jimmy Mitchell*

BEETS

A tree with green leaves and a brown bottom
A hundred snakes coming out of a basket
Four coconuts in a palm tree
An alien with four heads and three antennae
A cobweb duster
A lady with a hat and a dress but no head
A rocket with fire coming from the back
A paint brush with millions of hairs uncovering four heads
Four martians with thousands of legs tied together
A shooting star with green fire.

— *Suzanne Cope*

POEMS ABOUT PLACES

Robert Louis Stevenson provides a perfect example of the observant eye in his poem, "From a Railway Carriage." I like to use this poem to talk about the significance of getting down to details so that the reader can really see what you have seen, hear what you've heard, feel what you have felt.

FROM A RAILWAY CARRIAGE

Faster than fairies, faster than witches,
Bridges and houses, hedges and ditches;
And charging along like troops in a battle,
All through the meadows the horses and cattle
All of the sights of the hill and the plain
Fly as thick as driving rain;
And ever again, in the wink of an eye,
Painted stations whistle by.

Here is a child who clambers and scrambles,
All by himself and gathering brambles;
Here is a tramp who stands and gazes;
And there is the green for stringing the daisies!
Here is a cart run away in the road

Lumping along with a man and a load;
And here is a mill, and there is a river
Each a glimpse and gone for ever!

—*Robert Louis Stevenson*

The details in Stevenson's poem are supported by the hard-hitting rhymes and the energetic, driving rhythm. You can't help but hear the train and feel it roll swiftly down the tracks in this poem.

When we have read and talked about the poem, I ask the students to think of a special place in their lives and to describe what they see when they travel there. Here are some examples.

ALL BY A BEACH

I spy a starfish,
the feather of a bird,
thirty-one cents,
and a very sandy word,
a little baby's footprint,
a rattle with bells,
a crab, a fork,
and seven seashells,
all by a beach,
and all alone.

—*Andy Aronoff*

IN PAKISTAN

1. I walk through fields full of flowers
and across the bridge
and there the sailboats stay.

And there is my sailboat
near the blue water
near my house

2. In Pakistan in the deep woods
near the water across the bridge
and in the fields is my home. It's big
and has 5 rooms and a boat that's in my home.

3. In Pakistan I have a big house
that is nice and pretty.
In our country we clean our house every day.
That's the way we keep our home.

—Anjuman Kahn

Exercise 59

POEMS ABOUT FAMILIAR THINGS

Here is an exercise that worked very well with the youngest students – those in the second half of first grade. We looked at two poems about ordinary things that we see every day. Here they are:

THE TOASTER

A Silver-scaled Dragon with jaws flaming red
Sits at my elbow and toasts my bread.
I hand him fat slices, and then, one by one,
He hands them back when he sees they are done.

— *William Jay Smith*

MY NOSE

It doesn't breathe;
It doesn't smell;
It doesn't feel
So very well.

I am discouraged
With my nose:
The only thing it
Does is blows.

—*Dorothy Aldis*

We talked about how much fun these descriptions were
and about how poets use their imaginations. We talked a bit
about rhyme as well, and then we wrote about some familiar
things of our own.

MY MOP

My mop, my mop
reminds me of someone's hair
swooshing in the air.

—*Zoe Travis*

FEET

Stamp, stamp
Splish splash,
Slide, stop, walk
Up, down
Feet going
Up and down.

— *Talia Nachbi*

MY BED

My bed reminds
me of a cloud.
It's puffy, it's fluffy,

It's soft – ahhhhhhh.
It's very comfy.
Boing! Boing!
It's also bouncy.

—*Caroline Symon*

Exercise 60

I HAVE LIVED

Some of the student poems I have most admired were written in response to a poem that is more complicated than it may first appear to be:

I HAVE LIVED AND I HAVE LOVED

I have lived and I have loved;
I have walked and I have slept;
I have sung and I have danced;
I have smiled and I have wept;
I have won and wasted treasure;
I have had my fill of pleasure;
And all of these things were weariness,
And some of them were dreariness.
And all of these things – but two things –
Were emptiness and pain:
And Love – it was the best of them;
And Sleep – worth all the rest of them.

—*Anonymous*

The children take this poem very seriously, as an accounting of a life. We talk about what they have done in their own lives, and then we write.

P.E.A.C.E.

I have love and I have hate
I have black and I have white
　All together I have freedom

I have myself and I have others
I have my Dad and I have my Mom
We have fire and we have wind
We have love and we have friendship
We have paint and we have ink
We have heaven and we have hell
　We all have each other

I have blue and I have red
I have green and I have yellow
I have brown and I have black
　All together I have colors

I have life and I have death
I have war and I have peace
I have water and I have life
　We all have earth

　　　—Kristin Dobson

UNTITLED

I have worked and I have studied
I have read and I have written
I have added and divided
All these things are tedious

They sometimes make me delirious.
And all these things but
Two things
Were a terrible waste of time
And recess – the best of time
And P.E. – I'll take it anytime.

— *Paul Gordon*

EXAMPLES OF COMPLETED EXERCISES

Following are some examples of exercises completed by students who have taken class with me. They are included here to give you some idea of how other creative people have made use of some of the suggestions in this book.

EXERCISE 2: WHAT I LOVE

I LOVE TO DRAW
by Matthew Wahl

Producing the sounds of bombs and machine guns and explosions and crashes, my child lips sputtered and spit across the piece of paper which my pencil devoured. Drawing as fast as I could, I eagerly kept up with the way battle scenes unfolded in my mind. A tank comes across the line that represents a landscape, its gun pointed in the air. BOOM! A shot is fired up and a fast line from my pencil creates a streak across the page. It ends at a scribble where the plane I had drawn earlier is now in flames. KAPOW! The pilot descends from the heavens under his canopy of air. More similar actions occur on my no longer white page as the pencil lines and smudges build underneath my black graphite little hand. When the paper is saturated with marks, I toss it somewhere, anywhere, and grab a clean sheet from the stack on the floor.

As long as I can remember, I've always loved to draw. When I was probably 4 or 5, my parents bought me a little table and a little chair that I spent most of my days at scribbling away and drawing whatever popped up in my imagination, discovering new worlds locked away in generations of genes passed on to me, unconcerned that my sound effects overpowered the TV set.

Drawing battle scenes was always my favorite. I found myself in school many times having my drawings taken away by teachers. Or kids would often ask for them and I never hesitated to give them up.

I even remember the first time I discovered what the function of a compass was. I proudly drew circles and half circles on the wall above my bed. I would say they looked darn good for an 8-year-old, too, but my mother thought otherwise. Going through elementary school, all I can remember doing was daydreaming and drawing. And as long as I had that, I was content in my little world at the back of the class because my last name started with a "w," which, I guess, would explain why I participated in first grade twice. But I don't even remember that bothering me.

As I got older, my art evolved into more productive art. I started doing cover designs for yearbooks and science fairs, and I entered any contest that came my way. I designed a total of five t-shirts, two of which were for my high school and three for a summer camp where I worked. I also designed and collaborated with two other students on a mural to replace the 20-year-old mural in the office of my high school. I also painted another one on the wall of my art room. As a senior, I drew a comic for the school paper and continued to contribute up until the last days when I designed the cover of the graduation pamphlet that everyone received at the ceremony.

Throughout my short life I've probably drawn more pictures than one could imagine. But what's strange is that I never kept anything. I haven't any proof to validate any of this. When I filled a page, I'd have to grab a new one to let the story continue on and never thought once to hang on to any of it. The fun I got out of drawing when I was young wasn't from the final piece that Mom put up on the fridge. It was the process that kept me at the little table for so long.

EXERCISE 8:
ROOM WITH A VIEW

by Michaela Genitheim

I always loved rainy Sunday af-
ternoons in Vienna. I usually spent them In a coffeehouse in a
nice comfortable chair with a lot of magazines and newspapers
around me. The moment I entereed the place I could smell the
freshly roasted coffeebeans, hear the sizzling of the espresso
machine and the high clinky noise of the little silver spoons
against the china cups.

The waiter would bring over the "coffee menu" and I'd
order, as usual, a "Grosser Brauner," a strong coffee with cream.
Then I would walk over to the glass vitrine filled with pastries,
cookies and cakes. I always had a hard time deciding which
one to pick, but after five or ten minutes I usually was able to
make up my mind and would order two small pastries. On the
way back to the table, I picked up magazines and newspapers.
Finally I was able to lean back in my chair, to close my eyes
and just enjoy the atmosphere.

After a while the waiter would come over, to put a small
brown, oval tray in front of me. The coffee always had a nice
brown color and the chocolate pastries looked delicious. With
the coffee I also got a glass of water and a piece of chocolate.
What else would I need? It was perfect. The waiter left with-

out a word, leaving me alone to enjoy the coffee and my newspapers. Every once in a while he would come back to put a new glass of water on the table, and without a word, he would leave again.

I usually sat there for two to three hours. Nobody would ever think about putting my check on the table and asking me to leave. I was a guest and was treated as one.

I enjoyed the quiet atmosphere. I watched people coming and leaving, and sipped on my water. Sometimes friends would stop by. They'd say hello, sit down, grab some papers and slip off into their own little worlds.

No wonder that the best poetry and literature was written in these places. The most interesting conversation and discussions have taken place here, between famous Austrian artists, poets and actors.

When it started to get dark out, I would call the waiter over, pay my bill and leave.

EXERCISE 10:
A PLACE ALTERED BY MOODS

MAD IN *LOVE* WITH THE KITCHEN
by Felipe Lloreda

Anger...

I opened the door and a breeze of burned onions runs through my nose. It smells terrible. The whole apartment smells like a garbage truck. The kitchen looks as if a war has just taken place but with food as the bullets. My roommate has not helped with the kitchen. the garbage disposal is clogged. The pieces of rotten food are lying in the sink as if another was taking place down there. Pieces of potatoes floating, peeled onions roaming, rotten tomatoes sinking, and the water almost dying. It's disgusting. I can't even breathe. I open the windows but that doesn't help. The annoying odor begins to travel at fast speeds through the apartment, into the closets, our bedrooms, our clothes and the bathrooms. Soap and detergent haven't visited the apartment for a couple of weeks. It's unbelievable how a decent place can turn into a garbage dump in just a few weeks. I can't even walk barefoot on the kitchen floor. The grease makes it impossible. You could actually skate without the use of ice skates. Everything you touch has a residue of grease on it. I can't stand it. The stench of the kitchen is driving me crazy. I'm out of here...

Love...

I can smell the roasted chicken from the other end of the hall. I walk rapidly to my apartment and delicious smells make my stomach growl. I open the door and find my girlfriend chopping onions. The kitchen is clean and welcoming. It looks as if a professional housekeeper has just cleaned it. The wonderful aroma of baked potatoes and sauteed mushrooms invades the apartment. A feeling of coziness and love pervades the atmosphere. I glance through the oven window and admire the art of cooking. I'm hungry. Hungry for love and food. The table is set with candles, beautiful silverware, flowered plates and a bottle of red wine. The music in the background makes it even more romantic. Finally, dinner is served. What a pleasure. The pleasure of cooking with love. Everything is clean and spotless. The dishwasher doesn't make a sound. Dessert is served. The kitchen has surpassed the test of love.

EXERCISE 12:
OBSERVING A STRANGER

by Dena Massenburg

I was unsure whether he was homeless or not, as he leered across the cafe table. I checked his appearance for signs of some kind. His fingernails for dirt or cracks, his moustache for remnants of food, the air around him for that tell-tale odor. He was clean. Yet, he still seemed to exude that certain derelict something.

His bushy salt and pepper sprinkled eyebrows (or rather, "eyebrow," since they connected in the center) were barely visible beneath his tightly fitted cobalt blue beret, from which a few steel gray curls had escaped and set up residence upon his rather dainty little ears. His darting black eyes, buried beneath his brows, were perfectly centered above the deep dimple-like wrinkles that lined his cheeks. The only visible part of his mouth was his fleshy lower lip (the top was covered by his comical moustache), which looked more like a welt on his chin than anything else; it was a thin line of flesh, slightly puffy in the middle, pushed into the cleft of his chin, as if he were pouting. From the center of all this rose the only feature which veered from his resemblance to Oscar the Grouch, a classical Roman nose. The rest of his hulking figure was draped in an array of blue scarves and a drab green trench coat, which puddled on the floor around his immense work boots.

His features seemed to melt from anger to confusion, to a number of possible emotions. It was as if he felt these things all at once. Unable to portray his emotions simultaneously, he settled for showing them in rapid succession. His behavior was a bit odd, but it was nothing that warranted the impression that he might be a derelict.

The only aspect of the encounter that gave any validity to my doubts was the dialogue he spewed at no one in particular. The questions he asked were followed by a slight pause, then answered confidently by himself. Before I could get an idea of what he was talking about, he'd switch topics again. From what I gathered, he was once a pickpocket and a drug dealer, but had a desire to teach in the public school system. He'd traveled extensively throughout Sweden and South America and could only discuss their restrooms. My mind was abuzz with his wild rantings, but still craved more. Unfortunately, my observations were interrupted by the sight of a friend. As I packed up to leave, I caught his eye and smiled before greeting my friend. As we headed toward the door, I looked back once more. He was smiling quietly to himself. Then he continued his dialogue.

EXERCISE 17:
LETTER FROM A PLACE YOU'VE NEVER BEEN

by Chris Sprouls

Dear Susan,

It may sound strange but I'm writing this letter from the underworld... Yes, that's right, Hell. Just think: you've told me to go there so many times. Who would have thought I'd take the trip? I don't really remember too much after the car lost control and I was heading for that oncoming car. Next thing I know, this intense heat wakes me and I'm sitting at a table with two guys in three-piece suits. Took me a while to figure out I was dead, but when they told me they were looking over my life I got the hint. It seems that everyone really does have their own personal Hell.

After looking over my papers these guys became really pleasant and the temperature cooled down. They began asking me about myself, my likes, favorite places, and assured me I was a likely candidate for upstairs. This was very surprising,. As you know, I'm not the best egg in the carton. But, heck, I was glad to help out and to make my trip easier, turns out all the information I gave was used to find out what I hated. I'm writing this from the top of a roller coaster which has no safety belts and just sits on the edge at all times. I used to scream, puke and get the shakes but I'm used to it now. That means any minute those guys in suits will take me to another horrible place. I never thought I'd be used to Michael Bolton and shark attacks... Who knew? Anyway, I wish you were here and I know you don't miss me. I get to write this letter to the person I hurt the worst. I suppose that's so later I can see you read it and laugh as I cry... If so, I'd like to say screw you. I'd do it again. Got to go. Cockroach bath awaits.

Damned forever,

Mike

EXERCISE 26: WRITING FROM PHOTOGRAPHS AND PICTURES

by *Lorine Pergament*

I am still young enough to sleep in a crib. I am in my grandparents' house. I hear a lot of noise. It sounds like there are a lot of people beyond my bedroom door, but I can't find out because I am a prisoner. I hold onto the bars and pull myself up. I cry because I don't know what is happening and I am afraid. Into the white room comes a big smiling man with a red face. He says something soothing, but I don't know what it is... I am later told that it must have been Grandma's brother Louie. Thank you, Louie.

I am about two. My mother and I are walking down a path next to an open field. It is a warm day, and the sun is high in the sky and very bright. Mom and I sometimes hold hands and sometimes I run off to pick something interesting or pretty. The field is full of high grass and wildflowers. It is a very yellow day. Mom and I are both wearing summer dresses. Mine is pink or blue. Hers is a print. Later that day, my cousin Bonnie and I are supposed to be sleeping. We are in a hotel room. We talk and look out the window, but the view is a disappointing parking lot. No one is with us...

We are living in the veterans' housing project on North Munn Avenue in Newark. Mom takes me to kindergarten. I am only four and a half. Mom stays for a while on the first day, but I am not upset when she leaves. I remember the room with its little tables and chairs. I remember the teacher being nice. I think I liked kindergarten.

That summer I go to daycamp on a bus every day. There is a boy who likes me. He sits next to me on the bus, and one day he gives me a present. It is a costume jewelry pin that looks like a bumble bee. I am so surprised and happy. Mom is overwhelmed. Later he asks me to marry him, no kidding. Mom makes me a "wedding gown" out of an old dress of hers. It is white satin with royal purple trim. I feel like a princess when I wear it. We get married in the basement of my apartment house. There are some other kids there. I can't remember my groom's name or face....

EXERCISE 27:
THE AIRPLANE

CRIMINAL INTRODUCTION
by Scott Rier

———————

From the day that I was born I knew that I was destined to be a criminal. Right after I was forced out of my spot I was actually forced into stealing my mother's milk. She was quite rude about it. But I guess no one was looking.

That was only the beginning of my life-long career as a criminal. At the tender age of three, I was lured by my mother into stealing a package of grape bubblegum. She said it wasn't worth it, whatever that meant.

On my fifth birthday, I got the surprise of my life. We went to the local hardware store to look at bikes. We lifted the raddest looking Huffy Chopper. My mother actually told me she "had a tab." What did I know?

When I was in second grade, me and my mother met with the teacher about grades. She made me grab the teacher's red apple. She said the teacher was never going to eat it...I guess not!

When I was ten years old my mother taught me all about "these new machines." The next day in school I unlocked my very own Macintosh. From that day on I never got another bad report card in school.

When I was in junior high school things got kind of easy. One day in the variety store, she didn't even see me snag my first green bottle of Hefenreffer. By that age, everybody was drinking a forty ounce bottle of malt liquor.

Right after I passed my driving test, me and my mother went to look at cars. We test drove a brand new Mercedes Benz. I never took the car back. My friends and I had a great time with it in my garage.

Oh, I'm sorry. I don't believe my manners. This is my mother. This is our first time ever on a plane.....

EXERCISE 43:
THE DOOR IN THE WALL

by Felipe Lloreda

The door was freshly painted with a suave blue. It reminded me of the ocean. I opened it, and there it was: a beautiful place filled with flowers, trees and fields of grass. Greens, yellows, reds, oranges and other unimaginable colors could be found in this paradise. It is fresh and sunny. The sun was halfway out giving life to this astonishing place. The delicious smell of flowers brought me memories. It's lovely. It feels perfect. My mouth can taste the blueberries and Guayabas found in this tropical paradise. The mangos and apples hang from the trees ready to be tasted. The wild berries and juicy pears make my mouth watery. The streams and waterfalls can be heard from a far distance. It's mother nature. Waiting to be destroyed. It's all a dream. A dream that can be seen only once....

EXERCISE 53:
METAPHORICAL THINKING:

THE WIND
by Dave Rehor

The wind is a potent and agressive spirit that chills every vulnerable speck of unprotected skin. The ingredients in the wind can give life or take it away. It can dance around you in ritual mockery. It can caress you like a blanket or it can bring you to your knees. The wind is a symbol of change, the beginning of a new season, the coming of a storm, the erosion of the landscape. It is like Sheba: she can create and destroy, but no mortal has the power to control her. The wind can also symbolize pleasure and life by spreading fragrant incense over the dead hills. She can lift you up to your apogee of spirits. The wind is the vehicle for all earthly spirits, warm or cold. The wind is a vapor action cough drop for the soul.

SHARKS
by Sue Dowdall

———————

Sharks are graceful birds of the sea gliding endlessly through the depths of the ocean, searching for food and mates, their reasons for life. Kings of the ocean, they have no fear. They rule the seas, dominating the waves. Their sleek grey bodies are like torpedos that have just been fired. They swim with such determination, the water hardly touching their tough armored skin. With the cunning of a rodent they snatch their prey, with grace and ease. The seal is gone as if it were never there.

ANIMALS
by Mike West

Animals are like people without power. They have families, raise their young, gather in groups for protection, and have social hierarchies. They play and discover and work. They live off the land and each other. But as much as animals resemble humans, there is one key difference: power. People abuse power, desire power and kill for power. They control and destroy to reach an elevated form of being. They want more than nature has given to those who share a world full of creatures. People use their power over each other and over animals for gain. Animals simply share and survive, content with their status and place in the world.